COOL CARS

MASERATI MC20

BY KAITLYN DULING

EPIC

Bellwether Media ››› Minneapolis, MN

EPIC BOOKS are no ordinary books. They burst with intense action, high-speed heroics, and shadows of the unknown. Are you ready for an Epic adventure?

This edition first published in 2024 by Bellwether Media, Inc.

No part of this publication may be reproduced in whole or in part without written permission of the publisher. For information regarding permission, write to Bellwether Media, Inc., Attention: Permissions Department, 6012 Blue Circle Drive, Minnetonka, MN 55343.

Library of Congress Cataloging-in-Publication Data

Names: Duling, Kaitlyn, author.
Title: Maserati MC20 / by Kaitlyn Duling.
Description: Minneapolis, MN : Bellwether Media, 2024. | Series: Cool cars. | Includes bibliographical references and index. | Audience: Ages 7-12 | Audience: Grades 2-3 | Summary: "Engaging images accompany information about the Maserati MC20. The combination of high-interest subject matter and light text is intended for students in grades 2 through 7"–Provided by publisher.
Identifiers: LCCN 2023001647 (print) | LCCN 2023001648 (ebook) | ISBN 9798886875003 (library binding) | ISBN 9798886876888 (ebook)
Subjects: LCSH: Maserati automobiles--Juvenile literature. | Sports cars--Juvenile literature. | Automobiles--Juvenile literature.
Classification: LCC TL215.M34 D85 2024 (print) | LCC TL215.M34 (ebook) | DDC 629.222/2--dc23/eng/20230113
LC record available at https://lccn.loc.gov/2023001647
LC ebook record available at https://lccn.loc.gov/2023001648

Text copyright © 2024 by Bellwether Media, Inc. EPIC and associated logos are trademarks and/or registered trademarks of Bellwether Media, Inc.

Editor: Rachael Barnes   Designer: Jeffrey Kollock

Printed in the United States of America, North Mankato, MN.

TABLE OF CONTENTS

SPEED THROUGH THE SNOW	4
ALL ABOUT THE MC20	6
PARTS OF THE MC20	12
THE MC20'S FUTURE	20
GLOSSARY	22
TO LEARN MORE	23
INDEX	24

SPEED THROUGH THE SNOW ≫

Snow covers the narrow mountain roads. But the driver is not worried.

The Maserati MC20 easily grips the snowy roads. Its excellent **handling** makes the **supercar** easy to drive!

ALL ABOUT THE MC20

MASERATI HEADQUARTERS IN MODENA, ITALY

Maserati started in Italy in 1914. The company was founded by three brothers.

Today, Maserati makes **luxury** sports cars. The Alfieri and MC12 are famous **models**.

MC12

📍 WHERE IS IT MADE?

EUROPE

MODENA, ITALY

The MC20 first hit roads in 2021. It was Maserati's first supercar in more than 15 years. The number in its name stands for 2020. That was the year it was announced.

2020 MC20 ANNOUNCEMENT

MC20 BASICS

YEAR FIRST MADE — 2021

COST — starts at $217,000

HOW MANY MADE — up to 1,400 a year

FEATURES

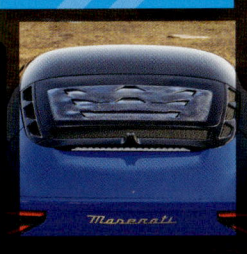
V6 Nettuno engine

butterfly doors

front grille with badge

The MC20 was built for the road rather than the racetrack. But it is still fast!

The supercar can reach 60 miles (97 kilometers) per hour in less than 3 seconds!

READY TO RACE

Maserati built the MC20 GT2 for the racetrack! This speedy model has just one seat. It comes with a fire extinguisher!

MC20 GT2

PARTS OF THE MC20 ≫

The MC20 uses a new type of engine made by Maserati. It is called Nettuno and is based on the build of a race car.

The powerful engine is paired with an eight-speed **automatic transmission**.

ENGINE SPECS

TWIN-TURBO V6 NETTUNO ENGINE ≫

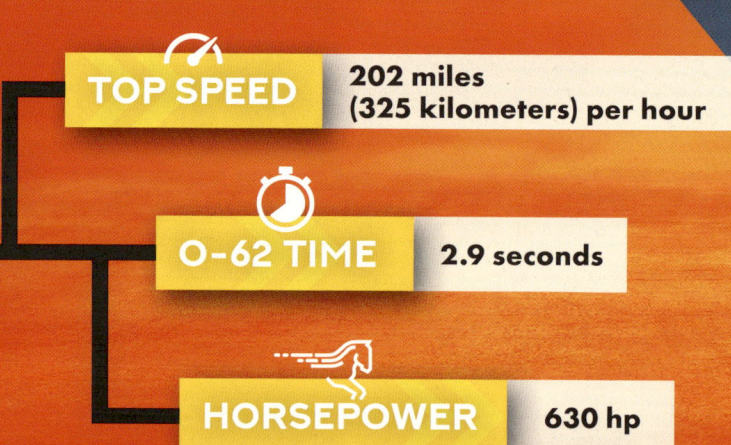

TOP SPEED	202 miles (325 kilometers) per hour
0-62 TIME	2.9 seconds
HORSEPOWER	630 hp

IN CONTROL

The MC20 has five driving modes. One mode helps the driver stay in control when it rains or snows. Another is for racing!

A **carbon fiber** body makes the MC20 lightweight. This helps the car speed down the road!

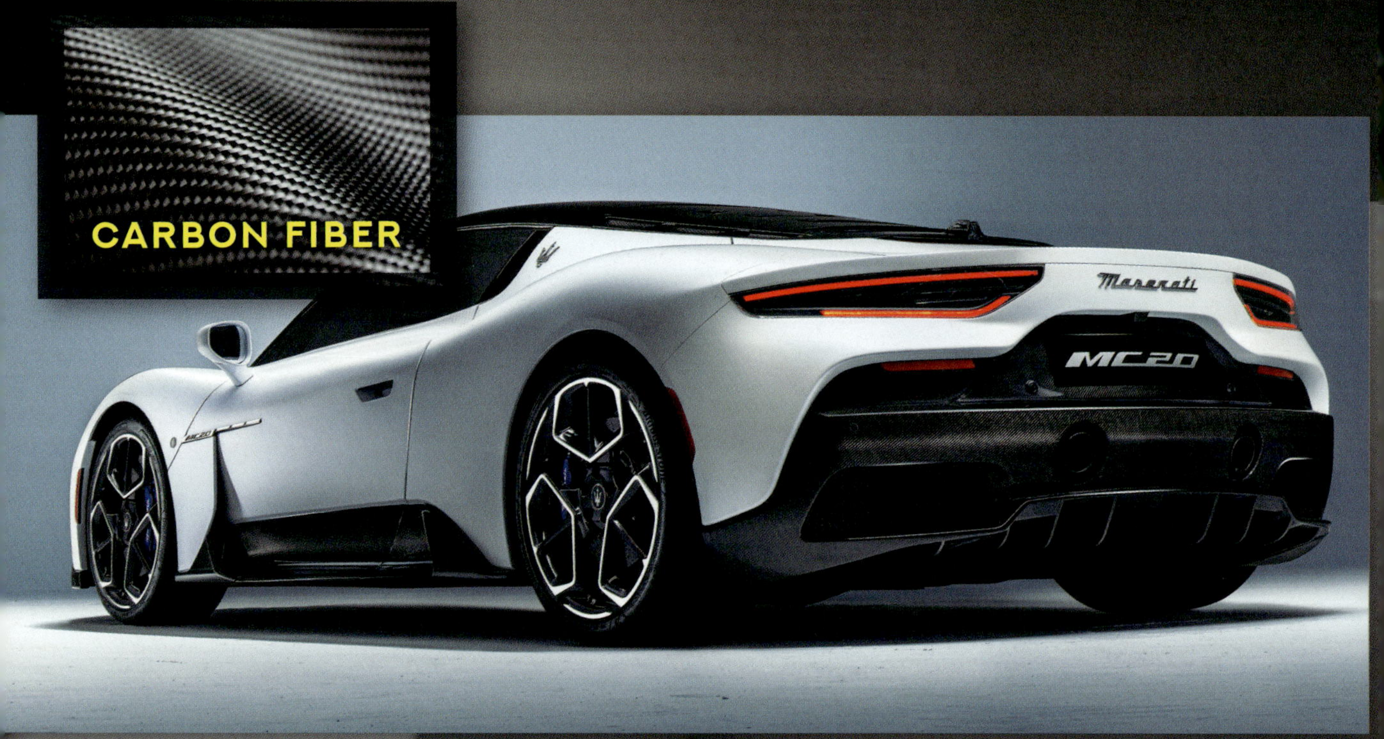

CARBON FIBER
Maserati
MC20

SIZE CHART

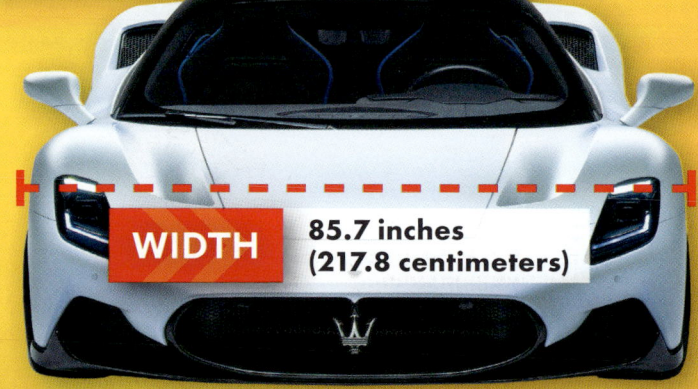

WIDTH
85.7 inches
(217.8 centimeters)

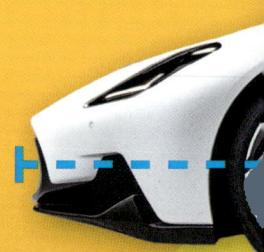

Carbon fiber also gives the car its unique shape. The car's smooth body is eye-catching!

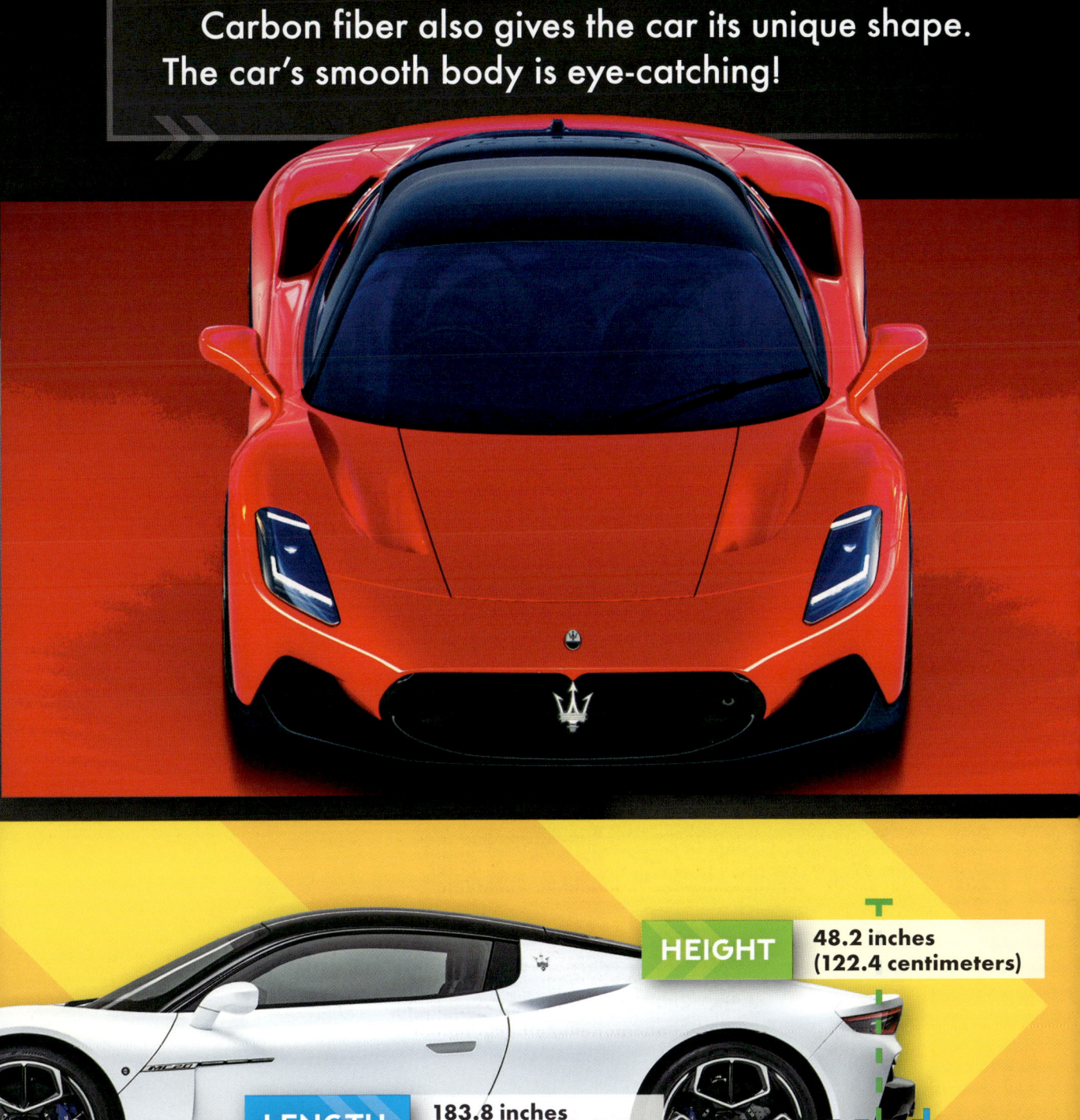

HEIGHT 48.2 inches (122.4 centimeters)

LENGTH 183.8 inches (466.9 centimeters)

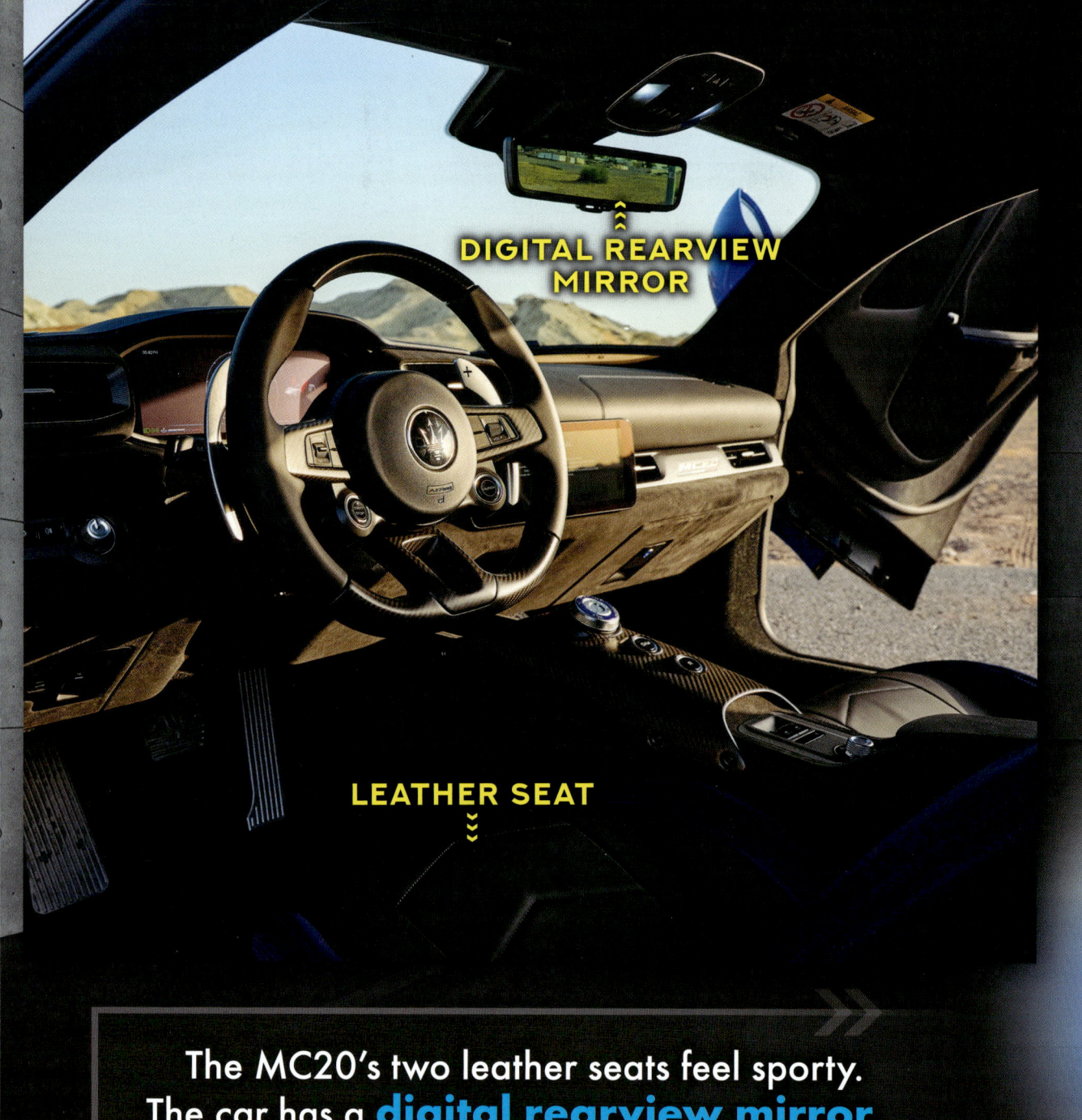

DIGITAL REARVIEW MIRROR

LEATHER SEAT

The MC20's two leather seats feel sporty. The car has a **digital rearview mirror**. This shows the rear camera view while driving.

Two **butterfly doors** open up and out. The front **grille** features a large **badge**.

BEHIND THE BADGE
All Maserati cars have the company's famous badge. It looks like the spear of Neptune, the powerful Roman god of the seas.

BADGE

‹‹‹ BUTTERFLY DOORS ›››

GRILLE

In 2022, Maserati announced the MC20 Cielo model. *Cielo* means "sky" in Italian.

MC20 CIELO

RETRACTABLE ROOF

The MC20 Cielo has a **retractable** glass roof. It can open to the sky in just 12 seconds!

THE MC20'S FUTURE »

Maserati plans to build an **electric** MC20 with **all-wheel drive**. The company wants all of its cars to be electric by 2030. Big changes are ahead for Maserati cars!

GLOSSARY

all-wheel drive—a system in a car that sends power from the engine to all four wheels

automatic transmission—a car part that shifts gears for the driver

badge—a sign to show that a person or thing belongs to a certain group

butterfly doors—car doors that open up and out like butterfly wings

carbon fiber—a strong, lightweight material used to strengthen things

digital rearview mirror—a mirror that shows the area behind a car using a rear camera

electric—able to run using electricity instead of gasoline

grille—a set of bars that cover an opening on the front of a car; the grille allows air to enter and exit.

handling—how a car performs around turns

luxury—related to having a high level of comfort

models—specific kinds of cars

retractable—able to be pulled back or inside

supercar—an expensive and high-performing sports car

TO LEARN MORE

AT THE LIBRARY
Colby, Jennifer. *Maserati*. Ann Arbor, Mich.: Cherry Lake Publishing, 2022.

Friesen, Helen Lepp. *Maserati*. New York, N.Y.: AV2, 2022.

Peterson, Megan Cooley. *Maserati GranTurismo*. Mankato, Minn.: Black Rabbit Books, 2021.

ON THE WEB

Factsurfer.com gives you a safe, fun way to find more information.

1. Go to www.factsurfer.com.

2. Enter "Maserati MC20" into the search box and click 🔍.

3. Select your book cover to see a list of related content.

INDEX

all-wheel drive, 20
automatic transmission, 12
badge, 17
basics, 9
body, 14, 15
brothers, 6
butterfly doors, 17
digital rearview mirror, 16
driving modes, 13
electric, 20
engine specs, 12
future, 20
grille, 17
handling, 5
history, 6, 8, 18
Italy, 6, 7
Maserati (company), 6, 7, 8, 11, 12, 17, 18, 20
models, 7, 11, 18, 19

name, 8, 18
Nettuno engine, 12
racetrack, 10, 11
roads, 4, 5, 8, 10, 14
roof, 19
seats, 16
size chart, 14–15
snow, 4, 5, 13
speed, 10, 11, 14
supercar, 5, 8, 11

The images in this book are reproduced through the courtesy of: Mike Mareen, front cover; Maserati, pp. 3, 4, 5, 8-9, 11, 12, 13, 14, 14 (width), 15, 15 (length), 17 (badge), 17, 18, 19, 20, 21; Travellaggio, p. 6; Max Earey, p. 7; NA, pp. 9, 9 (grille), 9 (doors), 9 (engine), 16; Annovi.frizio, p. 10; Composite_Carbonman, p. 14 (carbon fiber).